TO BE RICH IS NOT DIFFICULT

Unlock Your Hidden Values and Convert Them into Riches

ANTHONY ENU

TABLE OF CONTENTS

INTRODUCTION

One of the toughest challenges people face in life is financial instability, which often leads to poverty. Poverty is the state of being in lack of what you need and always desire things you can't afford. In contrast, riches flow abundantly, and there is never a shortage of wealth for those who have discovered their value. Your value is what makes you unique and desirable, and it can lead you to financial success beyond your wildest dreams. Everyone wants to be Rich and comfortable in Life, but the understanding of the inflow of riches is made known to few. If you must be rich, then you need to be free from confusion; Confusion is a state of depravity in humanity. Poverty, shame, lack, sickness and death is a state of confusion in a Man. Whatever that overcame a man first confused the Man outside his knowledge. Don't forget that lack of self-Discovery will eventually connect Men to the wrong path which leads to self destruction from valuelessnes. The Greatest miracle that can happen to you is to have an ability to understand what you are meant to know at every given time. Your ability to understand what you are meant to know at every given time is a Divine quality that produces riches. Poverty dwells anywhere darkness is found; the essence of light in your life is to produce a brightness that can outshine the darkness of poverty. Until men come to a realm where they live from the light of their life, poverty and death won't end.

It is the quality of brightness in your soul that declares your value before God. The value of Man is represented by his soul quality; to be rich will not be difficult if there is abundance of light in your soul. Satan makes so much effort to separate men from the path of their destiny through distraction and confusion. Have you wondered why people find it very hard to discover their life purpose early? Your greatness can only be found in the path of your Destiny. The Riches you seek should come from the path of your Purpose, any riches that you got outside the path of your purpose will eventually end your life in a bad way and may stop you from fulfilling your right purpose on Earth. Don't look for money first without Discovering and recovering your Value. It can be dangerous to pursue money without considering your value. Being wealthy is not hard if you have a valuable skill or trait that is in demand. The ability to convert your value into financial success is the key to achieving riches.

However, you cannot find money without first discovering yourself. A discovered life is a recovered Destiny. Those who abandon themselves and their values in pursuit of wealth often end up as victims of circumstance. Your life's purpose is defined by your unique value, and your value can lead you to greatness, but it takes discipline to keep you on the right path.

Being rich is not difficult if you have something useful to offer. Being relevant is what makes you important, and until you become important, you cannot declare your worth. Remember, your value is what will lead you to financial success, and a disciplined character will keep you there. The worth of a person can be translated into wealth; becoming rich is not difficult if you use the value that you have discovered within yourself and direct it towards the right path. Who you are becoming is more significant than who you used to be. A person's transformation can only be achieved from within through self-discovery. All transformed lives are discovered lives and All discovered lives are recovered Destinies.

As you pursue through the pages of this book, you will gain a wealth of knowledge and experience steps to financial abundance. Make it a priority to read and share with others. May God bless you.

CHAPTER 1

TO BE RICH IS NOT DIFFICULT

Financial instability is a significant challenge that

people often face, leading to poverty and a state of lack. However, it's imperative to remember that riches flow abundantly, and discovering your value can undoubtedly pave the way to affluence. The discovery of your value is a powerful selling point that can open doors to abundance, and you can convert it into wealth with the right direction.

It's essential to focus on who you are becoming rather than who you used to be. Who you used to be is your past and who you are becoming is your future. Transformation can be possible through self-discovery, and you must maintain the value associated with riches to keep a steady inflow of money. It's crucial to remember that self-discovery is key when chasing after money, as neglecting it can lead to disaster.

Everyone has a unique ability that can attract what they need, but you must discover it and live from it. Sufficiency is guaranteed for those who discover their self-value, and your uniqueness and peculiarity should never be ignored. Neglecting self-value is a surefire way to make it difficult to become rich and eventually leads to self- abandonment and living for the wrong purpose. Therefore, you must prioritize your self-discovery and confidently pursue your path to affluence.

SELF ABANDONMENT LEADS TO POVERTY

Poverty is the result of lack of self-discovery. Pursuing money without understanding oneself can lead to disastrous consequences. However, when people truly understand their values and potentials and live by them, they can achieve true riches that positively impact their world. Living for the wrong purpose leads to poverty, which is a state of insufficiency and an inability to afford basic necessities. In contrast, living for a meaningful purpose that aligns with one's values and principles leads to a fulfilling life.

Being rich means possessing the ability to understand one's purpose and being disciplined enough to pursue it. Poor people often lack self-value, which leads to a poverty mindset. However, by recognizing their inherent value and embracing self-discovery, people can achieve success and happiness.Poverty is a state of mind that is often rooted in fear, doubt, and limiting beliefs. Poor people tend to have a poverty consciousness that holds them back from achieving their full potential. By adopting a growth mindset and embracing self-discovery, people can overcome these limiting beliefs and achieve greatness.

Every person has a God-given value that can lead to a fulfilling life. Self-discovery is the key to unlocking this potential and living a life of purpose. When people understand their true value, they can recover their destiny and achieve greatness. The God of every man is introduced from his self-value. The self-value of a man is a discovered potential that makes up the man and declares his earth relevance; everyone is introduced to relevance through his discovered self-value from the potential of his usefulness. All forms of greatness are connected to usefulness; your ability to be relevant on earth is your qualification for greatness.

22 And Saul sent to Jesse, saying, Let David, I pray thee, stand before me; for he hath found favor in my sight.

23 And it came to pass, when the evil spirit from God was upon Saul, that David took an harp, and played with his hand: so Saul was refreshed, and was well, and the evil spirit departed from him. (1 Samuel 16: 22-23)

Greatness has an undeniable ability to inspire those who come in contact with it to discover their own value. David's usefulness to King Saul was a direct result of the unique value he brought to the table. The connecting point to relevance is value. This is a powerful reminder that you too have the potential to discover your own value, and offer it to the world with confidence.

When people give up on themselves, they often look to others for help. However, relying solely on the help of others can lead to a cycle of dependency. It's important to recognize that the best help you can give yourself is the help that comes from within yourself. Instead of simply giving people money, focus on providing value to their lives. When you give someone value, you're helping them to become self-sufficient and empowered. This is much more valuable than any amount of money you could give them. Remember, you have the power to offer true value, and that is a gift that will always be in high demand.

MONEY IS AN ATTRACTION

Money is a product of the value that you need to discover and harvest within yourself. Therefore, it is imperative to look for money within your discovered and harvested value, and it is futile to search outside of it. Those who have lost their lives in the pursuit of money were deceived into following the wrong path. The reason Africa is poor is that Africans abandoned their self-value and thought that going abroad to seek money would make them rich. However, any form of riches that isn't self-produced will always lead to poverty. Money is magnetic and has a formidable attraction force. It comes to those who can attract it and sustain it. The attractive force of money is driven by a reliable source of productivity. Therefore, having money is one thing, but sustaining it is another. Money is sustained from its reproductive value, and those who wish to have it must have the capacity to maintain it. Having money does not make you rich unless you have built a fortress of abundance from a sustainable source. Money comes to those who have what it takes to get it and stay with those who have developed a substantial capacity to uphold it. In essence, the more you look for money, the less you find it, as it is like air - always present, but only noticeable when you have a substantial capacity to attract and uphold it.

MONEY IS SUSTAINED THROUGH WISE INVESTMENT

Investment is the cornerstone of wealth creation. To amass and maintain wealth, one must continue to invest without hesitation. The most valuable investment you should embark on is self-investment, self investment is a process of self development and refining of self-value. By investing in yourself, it is guaranteed to reap the benefits of abundance and riches through your self harvest.Becoming wealthy is a matter of making wise investments and developing one's self-value. Successful individuals are those who have invested in themselves and have become proficient and excellent in their field. By investing in oneself, one can establish a solid foundation that provides all the necessary resources for a prosperous life. A person's usefulness is determined by their relevance, and relevance is achieved through shrewd investment. By investing money appropriately in the right direction, one can save money and multiply resources exponentially. To become wealthy, you must invest in yourself, become a money magnet, and allow money to flow through you from your self harvested Value.

Money can only flow through those who have discovered and developed their self-value. To become rich, one must cultivate the value within and make oneself an irresistible channel for money to flow through. By investing in yourself, you can become a money magnet and achieve financial abundance with confidence.

MONEY MULTIPLIES WHEN INVESTED WISELY

Becoming rich is a step-by-step process that begins with attracting money through self-harvesting.

However, merely accumulating money won't make you rich. Instead, wise and resultful investments are what will get you there. Those who have harvested their self value never lack what they need. When you invest your money properly in the right direction, it multiplies and grows exponentially. But beware, the danger of losing money and becoming poor is always present when making the wrong investment. It's crucial to avoid investing in uncertain ventures. Life involves taking risks, but some risks are better left unexplored due to the potential negative consequences.

If you focus on investing your money in the right direction, it will yield great returns in due time, and becoming rich will be well within your reach.

6. But this I say, He which soweth sparingly shall reap also sparingly, and he which soweth bountifully shall reap also bountifully.

(2 Corinthians 9:6)

DON'T ABANDON YOURSELF

Discovering your potential is a divine Ability, bestowed upon you by God. It's unfortunate how some people choose to abandon themselves and seek fulfillment from external sources. To abandon oneself is to disregard one's own credibility and settle for a mediocre existence. Poverty, in its first form, arises from self-abandonment. Those who abandon themselves live outside their true selves, and as a result, fail to achieve their full potential. Your true self is what gives you relevance, and anyone who lives outside of it cannot achieve greatness on earth. To become rich, one must first discover their true self and live in it. It is from this that life's purpose is defined and greatness is attained. So, let us all embrace our true selves and boldly pursue our life's purpose with confidence and determination.

38 For I came down from Heaven, not to do my own will, but the will of him that sent me. (John 6: 38)

20 I am crucified with Christ: nevertheless, I live; yet not I, but Christ liveth in me: and the life which I now live in the flesh I live by the faith of the Son of God, who loved me and gave himself for me.

(Galatians 2:20)

Understanding the purpose of your life is the key to unlocking endless riches, and living for the right purpose is the ultimate measure of success. Knowing the spirit that drives you forward not only enhances your life, but also secures your destiny. Aimless wandering on earth can lead to a lack of direction and purpose, but when you define the purpose of your life, you are on the path to achieving greatness. Don't abandon yourself in search of money, as this can lead to losing yourself altogether. So, take charge of your life, define your purpose, and success will surely follow.

CHAPTER 2

EVERY MAN WAS BORN TO BE RICH

Birth is the ultimate introduction to a world of

endless possibilities. We should understand that the very first step towards success and prosperity is a safe and healthy delivery into this world. I am certain that a person's destiny is determined by the circumstances of their birth.

Many great people have started their journey towards success and greatness from the moment they were born. Poverty is not a life sentence, it is simply the result of undervaluing oneself or negligence to self-value. True riches come from discovering one's value and purpose in life, and I believe that every person has the potential to achieve greatness through their discovered self.I am convinced that being alive is the greatest opportunity that life can offer us. It is a privilege that should never be taken for granted. I strongly believe that the relevance of a person's life starts from birth. One's destiny is closely tied to the purpose of their existence, which is often shrouded in the mystery of their birth. Sadly, those who do not survive birth are denied the chance to fulfill their destiny. But those who are born into this world are given the potential to achieve greatness.

In conclusion, I assert that riches are not just about material possessions. They are about discovering one's true worth and purpose in life. Every person has the potential to achieve greatness, and it all starts with understanding the importance of their birth and the opportunities that life presents. The destiny of a Man is introduced from his place of birth and can be harvested through self discovery. All forms of greatness are unique and can't be found everywhere.

The mystery in the birth of Jesus is a revelation that greatness is ordained right from birth; understanding the mystery behind your birth will give you a clarity of who you are or who you represent.

10 When they saw the star, they rejoiced with exceeding great joy. 11 And when they had come into the house, they saw the young Child with Mary His mother, and fell down and worshiped Him. And when they had opened their treasures, they presented gifts to Him: gold, frankincense, and myrrh. (Matthew 2:10-11)

NAMES ARE ASSOCIATED TO RICHES

A great destiny is always accompanied by a great name. Your name is a crucial aspect of defining your character and can act as a catalyst in determining your success. While some names are associated with success, others might be associated with failure. Therefore, it's imperative to understand the significance of your name as it is believed that spirits attach names to destinies. Your name is an integral part of who you are, and neglecting its meaning can lead to self-neglect. Those who ignore the significance of their name may not be able to fulfill their destiny, as your destiny is undoubtedly connected to your name. Hence, it's crucial to understand the meaning of your name as it is your first responsibility on earth.

9 And Jabez was more honorable than his brethren: and his mother called his name Jabez, saying, Because I bear him with sorrow.

10 And Jabez called on the God of Israel, saying, Oh that thou wouldest bless me indeed, and enlarge my coast, and that thine hand might be with me, and that thou wouldest keep me from evil, that it may not grieve me! And God granted him that which he requested.

(1 Chronicles 4:9_10)

Having a good name is one of the ways to achieve wealth and success in life. Great men like Jesus and John the Baptist were given their names by God, because Their greatness is attached to their name. Your name determines the height of your greatness on Earth, as names introduce men to their destiny. If you ignore self-knowing, self-denial will not end. Knowing your name is the first step to knowing yourself and your purpose. Names are very important because they carry the Angel of your destiny. All great spirits that manifested on earth in human form were introduced from the strength of their name. Therefore, the greatness of a man can be seen from the strength of his name.

31 And behold thou shalt conceive in your womb come on and bring forth a son, And shall call his name JESUS.

(Luke 1: 31)

God will consider your name before giving you a destiny.

13 But the Angel said unto him, fear not, Zacharias: for thy prayer is heard; and thy wife Elizabeth shall bear a son, and thou shall call his name John.

(Luke 1:13)

Aspiring for wealth is a commendable goal that many people strive towards. Having your name associated with success and cultivating self-assurance can be valuable assets as you navigate towards achieving financial prosperity.

SPIRITS MAKE MEN GREAT THROUGH THEIR NAME

28 And he said, Thy name shall be called no more Jacob, but Israel: for as a prince hast thou power with God and with men, and hast prevailed.

(Genesis 32:28)

Having a great name is a fundamental element of achieving greatness. It is believed that before God walks with anyone, He considers their name, and may even bestow upon them a better one. As individuals progress with God and their purpose, He may reveal a new name that reflects their potential and future success.

Negative connotations attached to one's name can hinder success and lead to a lack of abundance. It is vital to recognize that names have power and the name one bears has significance not only to God but to those around them. By associating one's name with their destiny, their path to success becomes clearer. A strong name is the foundation for achieving wealth and prosperity.

4 As for me, behold, my covenant is with thee, and thou shalt be a father of Many Nations.

5 Neither shall thy name any more be called Abram, but their name shall be Abraham; for a father of Many Nations have I made thee. (Genesis 17: 4-5)

If you haven't received a new name in your spiritual journey towards prosperity, ask God for one. A good name is valuable for attaining wealth.

SOUND MIND IS AN ASPECT OF RICHES

To have a productive mindset, having a sound mind is crucial. And a productive mindset leads to a rich mindset. Creativity is a state of mind that reflects its productive abilities, which is essential for success. Therefore, it's imperative to have a rich mindset as it is the product of a sound mind, which ultimately leads to success.

7 For God had not given us the spirit of fear; but of power, and sound mind.

(2 Timothy 1:7)

Having a sound mind is an essential key to acquiring wealth. The ability to think and act appropriately is only possible with a healthy mind. When the mind is stable and clear, riches will come effortlessly.

Witchcraft often targets people's minds, causing doubts and confusion. However, a sound mind is achieved by investing in learning and discrete knowledge. With a discreet knowledge of wealth, becoming rich becomes inevitable.

Developing a sound mind for a particular purpose is more important than praying and fasting for it. If the mind is sound, becoming rich in thought will not be difficult. In fact, being rich will become more attainable with a well-functioning and productive mind.

CHAPTER 3

RICHES ARE CONVERTED VALUE IN MEN

It is important to realize that your value is what can

help you generate money when utilized properly. Value is the product of a discovered potential within you, and if you learn how to convert it, becoming rich can become much easier.

Being productive is an essential aspect of value. It is important to declare your usefulness and relevance to your environment, which can help you be more productive and ultimately bring you closer to wealth. Your relevance is directly proportional to your value, so it is important to avoid becoming rich outside of your value, as that can lead to reaping where you did not sow. It is vital to allow your value to bring you to the gate of riches. Poverty is often the result of a lack of usefulness and relevance. Disregarding your self-value can lead to a decrease in productivity and ultimately a devaluing of yourself. To end poverty, you need to be useful and relevant to your environment and society. Furthermore, it is essential not to burden others by constantly sharing your problems with them. This can reduce your self-worth before them and make you appear valueless.

The importance of a person always speaks, even in their absence. Your impact on people declares your importance to them. It is important to become important to yourself and the people around you, as this is a unique path to abundant riches. Without becoming important and relevant, shame and mockery are inevitable. Therefore, focus on being productive, useful, and relevant to your environment, and success and fulfillment will follow.

THE STRENGTH OF FOCUS

Focus is a driven force from a discovered vision; it can only take a discovered vision to birth focus. The strength of focus is in consistently looking in a proper and particular direction.

2 Looking unto Jesus the author and finisher of our faith; who for the joy that was set before him endured the cross, despising the shame; and is set down at the right hand of the throne of God. (Hebrews 12: 2) Whatever you keep looking at will eventually transform you. The first transformation of a Man starts from what he is seeing. Every great deed attained was possible through the strength of focus. All Great achievers are visionary-minded.

To be focused will not be difficult if there is clarity of vision. Unless vision is defined, confusion is inevitable.

2 *And the Lord answered me, and said, Write the vision, and make it plain upon tables, that he may run that readeth it.*

3 *For the vision is yet for an appointed time, but at the end, it shall speak, and not lie: though it tarries, wait for it; because it will surely come, it will not tarry.*

(Habakkuk 2: 2-3)

All visionary-minded will eventually arrive at their destination as long as they remain on the path.

The Two Enemies Of Focus Are:

1. DISTRACTION

2. CONFUSION

DISTRACTION:

Distraction is a major obstacle to achieving focus, and it can cause significant delays in our lives. Every individual's life follows a particular path, and success can be achieved by staying on that path. Satan often tries to distract people from their path of destiny with various temptations. Distractions can take many forms, but their goal is to divert our minds and eyes from the right path.

3 And when the tempter came to him, he said, if thou be the Son of God, command that these Stones be made bread.

4 But he answered and said, It is written, Man shall not live by bread alone, but by every word that proceedeth out of the mouth of God.

(Matthew 4:3-4)

It's truly inspiring to see how Jesus was able to resist the temptation of the enemy by preparing himself and staying focused. We all know how easy it can be to lose our way when our minds are distracted and our hearts are deceived. That's why it's so important to maintain a clear and resolute mind that is free from any distractions. When we stay focused and give our all to God, we can achieve so much more. Even when we face discouragement or feel overwhelmed, it's important to stay confident and assertive in our pursuit of success. By keeping our focus on our goals and maintaining maximum concentration, we can overcome any obstacle and emerge victorious.

CONFUSION:

It can be tough to deal with confusion as it can leave us feeling lost and unfocused. When we're confused, it can be hard to make sense of things, and we may find ourselves considering options that don't align with our true selves. Unfortunately, this can be a real obstacle to achieving our goals and living a fulfilling life. It's important to recognize that confusion can be difficult to overcome, but with patience and divine guidance, it's possible to find our way back to clarity of purpose.

7 **For God had not given us the spirit of fear; but of power, and sound mind.**

(2 Timothy 1:7)

The spirit of confusion opens the door to fear and fear leads to death. Satan delights most in getting men confused and all confused men don't have God in them. To be confused in life is to stop hearing from God and when a Man stops hearing, the gate of doom will be widely open.

One of the ways to overcome confusion is to stay on track at all times, the pathway to great places is made from a focused mind. Satan makes much effort to get men confused in order to remove them from track, but the Spirit of Wisdom brings men into a state of excellence through proper guidance. All that got distracted and confused missed a step in the path of their destiny.

All confused lives are subdued lives, the path that leads to greatness should not be walked with the eyes of confusion. When the vision is not clear, men are liable to be doomed.

THE DANGER OF CONFUSION

Having clarity of vision is essential to avoid the dangers of confusion. Confusion leads to spiritual and mental blindness that stems from lack of knowledge. However, with a determined and focused mind, confusion can be sidestepped. It's easy to get overwhelmed by frustration, but you can stay on course with confidence and purpose. Frustration can be a roadblock that causes shame, regret, and even shortening of one's lifespan. Nonetheless, by having a clear understanding of the path to take and remaining committed to it, you can avoid confusion and reach your destination with confidence and ease.

GOD MAKES MEN RICH THROUGH THE CHANNEL MEN CREATES

1 **Blessed is the man that walketh not in the counsel of the ungodly, nor standeth in the way of sinners, nor sitteth in the seat of the scornful.**

2 **But his delight is in the law of the Lord; and in his law doth he meditate day and night.**

3 **And he shall be like a tree planted by the rivers of water, that bringeth forth his fruit in his season; his leaf also shall not wither; and whatsoever he doeth shall prosper.   (Psalms 1:1-3)**

If you desire prosperity, then you must create a path for it to flow through. Relying solely on God to provide

43

prosperity without taking any action is a waste of time. God created Man in his image and likeness to be creative and responsible, just like Him. Therefore, attaining true prosperity requires a partnership between God and Man. You have a role to play in creating a path for prosperity to flow. Every form of prosperity must pass through a channel created by Man. Simply asking God to bless you without creating the means for the blessing is unfair to God and hinders your own progress. So, take action today and create the channel for your prosperity to flow through.

God passes through the channel we have created for him in order to make us Rich. Any form of Riches that didn't pass through a given and sustainable channel will eventually vanish within the space of time. God is more interested in what we will give him than what he can give us, taking from God doesn't make you Rich, but giving to God will multiply your Riches. Which channel for prosperity have you created for God to pass through? If you have created a channel of prosperity, bringing God to pass through it won't be difficult.

CHAPTER 4

CONVERTING YOUR VALUE INTO RICHES

It's crucial to recognize that you hold immense value as an individual, and money is a powerful tool for exchanging that value with others. If you aim to become wealthy, you must focus on building a life that offers something invaluable to others. Strive to become the person that people can't do without, and you will enhance your relevance and demonstrate your worth with confidence. Always remember that success is a journey that takes time and understanding, and you must have unwavering belief in yourself and your abilities.

One of the most effective ways to achieve greatness is by being useful to others. To become a valuable asset to yourself and those around you, you must provide solutions to problems. Individuals who can provide assistance to others are highly respected, so be the one who provides answers to people's needs with confidence. It is crucial to invest in yourself and your skills, so you can be a boon to others. By becoming an asset to the world, you will find that wealth and success will gravitate towards you with confidence.

ATTRACTING RICHES FROM YOUR DISCOVERED VALUE

Investing in your own proficiency will yield sustainable outcomes over time. Your relevance to the Earth is what determines your legacy, and the Earth supports humanity, sustaining their memory long after they pass. It is essential to focus on productivity before seeking attention. Through productivity, you can attract what you need. You were created to live by yourself, but it is also important to consider differences and not depend on others for survival. Slavery is a form of self-abandonment, and it is crucial to recognize and respect the autonomy of every individual. Your value can only attract what you need if you are productive enough. Investing time in self-development is invaluable and may be more rewarding than seeking recognition. Your productivity is a testament to your greatness, and it is important to recognize and appreciate the unique contributions of every individual. If purpose must be accomplished, then confusion must be dealt with.

Ways To Overcome Confusion

- **Have a clear understanding of vision.**
- **Discover the right path of your vision and always stay on track.**

- Be prayerful and equipped spiritually through the word of God.
- Obtain the strength of focus
- Keep the right association with vision-minded
- Keep moving.

WAYS OF CONVERTING YOUR VALUE TO RICHES

1) SELF DISCOVERY

2) SELF DEVELOPMENT

3) SELF IMPROVEMENT

4) SELF DISCIPLINE

5) GET RIGHT SUPPORT.

SELF DISCOVERY:

Self-discovery is the key to becoming self-aware of your being and potential. It leads to self-recovery and until you discover yourself, you cannot unlock your full potential. Everything you uncover about yourself is already a part of you, waiting to be discovered. Every discovered life is a recovered destiny, and greatness lies in the path of discovery. The riches you seek are already within reach, waiting to be discovered and claimed. Your value must be recognized by yourself, as all valuable lives are discovered. What have you discovered about yourself? The greatness of every person is hidden in their value, and what sets you apart from others is what you know about yourself personally. There is a unique potential of God in you, and an innate ability that sets you apart and makes you special. Self-attention is the pathway to self-discovery, and waiting for a miracle to fall from heaven is not the solution. Whatever you want from God is already within you, and until you discover yourself, you cannot unlock your full potential and achieve greatness. So go ahead, discover yourself, and unlock your full potential.

SELF DEVELOPMENT:

In order to achieve greatness, it's important to discover your path and invest in yourself through self-development. Without investing in yourself, your potential and abilities may remain limited.

Jesus serves as an excellent example of this principle. Even though he discovered his purpose when he was incarnated by Christ, he waited 30 years to develop himself before entering into ministry. He used his experiences and struggles to prepare himself for his purpose.

If you don't develop your abilities, you may find yourself exposed before the right time. However, if you use the waiting period to build your capacity, you'll be better equipped to sustain yourself in times of trouble.

In today's world, many people are in a rush to be noticed and accepted. However, it's important to remember that your level of acceptance is determined by your readiness to remain at climax. By taking the time to develop your gift and fully prepare, you'll be able to create a greater impact. Rushing to fulfill purpose unprepared, on the other hand, may result in a limited impact that will easily be forgotten.

SELF IMPROVEMENT:

15 Study to shew thyself approved unto God, a workman that needeth not to be ashamed, rightly dividing the word of truth.

(2 Timothy 2:15)

Self-improvement is essential and crucial in achieving perfection and excellence. The process of self-improvement involves building on discovered and developed values. To attain excellence, all self-development must be self-improved. The journey of self-improvement requires patience and approval. There is no rush in destiny, and the path to achieving great destiny is a process that demands time. Self-improvement is a vital tool that keeps you on the right track. While it is good to be good, it is better to be the best, and the best lives are those that are self-improved. Don't stop at self-development, but make conscious efforts to improve your developed self. When you do this, excellence will lead you to the gate of riches.

SELF-DISCIPLINE:

Achieving greatness demands self-discipline, as grace alone cannot sustain one at the top. Self-discipline is the inner strength that empowers one to control oneself and make the right choices at all times. Those lacking self-discipline will stray from the path of success and ultimately suffer the consequences. The discipline you cultivate within yourself is your preparation for greatness, and it is a vital prerequisite for self-preservation. Successful people have a well-developed sense of self-discipline, while those who lack it will never attain or sustain wealth. Remember, self-discipline is the key to achieving greatness and retaining your position at the top.

GET RIGHT SUPPORT:

5 And I looked, and there was none to help; and I wondered that there was none to uphold: therefore my own arm brought salvation unto me; and my fury, it upheld me. (Isaiah 63:5)

Receiving support from others is incredibly valuable, but it's important to remember that the most meaningful support often comes in the form of attention and care. Those who give you their attention and time are the ones who will be there for you when you need financial assistance. Life can be challenging, and we all need help from others and from a higher power to reach our goals. That being said, the support we give to ourselves is just as important as the support we receive from others. Even when life doesn't provide everything we need, having faith in ourselves can inspire us to keep going. To find the right support from others, it's crucial to surround ourselves with like-minded individuals who share our vision and dreams. Simply being around people who believe in us can provide us with the support we need, even when we don't realize it. It's natural to feel let down when people disappoint us, but it's important not to lose hope. Disappointment can be a message to become more self-sufficient, but it's also true that every great success story is built on the foundation of strong support. May you find the people and the support you need to fulfill your destiny, and may God guide you on your journey.

GROW IN WHAT YOU ALREADY KNOW

Life presents us with endless opportunities to advance, and true advancement stems from continuous improvement. Every time we advance, we improve our lives and the values we hold dear. We are destined for greater heights, and that's why we cannot remain where we are. Greatness demands that we seek and embrace greater levels of advancement.

So keep growing in what you already know and never stop advancing. The key to unlocking your best self lies in self-advancement. It's only by advancing yourself that you can attain the knowledge and skills you need to reach your full potential.

CHAPTER 5

ALL RICH MEN ARE MEN OF VALUE

The level of attention people will give you is directly proportional to the positive impact you make in their lives. Successful individuals possess immense value that leads them to reign supreme. A man's value opens the gateways to riches and abundance. Productivity determines your worth, and all individuals with value are highly productive. It is not the possession of wealth that makes one rich, but being useful and relevant that ensures your name and legacy are remembered. Some people acquire wealth through various means, but remain useless and irrelevant to their society. True success comes from being relevant. People don't respect you because you have money; they respect and honor you because of the immense value you bring. Action speaks louder than words, but value speaks louder than money. Instead of chasing money, focus on discovering your value and positively impacting the world.

God relies on the value of men to reign on earth. Christ's value made him great. When Jesus was a carpenter, there was little attention paid to his relevance and importance, but when he manifested God's Glory, the world followed him because of his impact.

54 When he came into his own country, he taught them in their synagogue, insomuch that they were astonished, and said, Whence hath this man this wisdom and these mighty works?

55 Is this not the carpenter's son? Isn't his mother called Mary? And his brethren, James, and Joses, and Simon, and Judas?

56 And his sisters, are they not all with us? Whence then hath this man all these things?

57 And they were offended by him. But Jesus said unto them, A prophet is not without honor, save in his own country, and his own house. (Matthew 13:54-57)

All the best in the world have a representation of their Value that declared their greatness; and through consistent self-improvement, they came to the limelight of riches from their place of Value. Whenever you remember a great man, his deeds will come before you. There is always an earth representation of a Man; the earth representation of every man can not be separated from their Value through a dedicated achievement. All Rich Men are Men of Value because their Riches flow from their earth relevance. Africans can never finish with Aliko Dangote because he has so much productivity from his discovered value which advances the human race. The only way you can be too important to people is when you have what they need and the moment you reduce from being useful, you lose your value.

DON'T SIT ON YOUR VALUE

Your worth is determined by what you have achieved. Don't overlook it. Discovering your true self leads to self-recovery, which is the greatest miracle of all. Those who disregard their value will end up with nothing. It's a great blessing to realize your true potential and fulfill your destiny. We all get lost at some point, but it's our responsibility to try and find ourselves. Failing to do so is denying ourselves the opportunity to be relevant. Everyone has something to offer, but we need to recognize and appreciate our value.

14 Neglect, not the gift that is in thee, which was given thee by prophecy, with the laying on of hands by the presbytery.   (1 Timothy 4:14)

Self neglect will eventually end In self-abandonment and every self-neglected life will never live purposely. To sit on your Value is to abandon yourself and self-abandonment leads to poverty.

THE UNIQUENESS OF EVERY VALUE

It's important to remember that your uniqueness is what sets you apart and makes you truly outstanding. You possess strengths and abilities that no one else can replicate. Embracing and understanding your worth is key to unlocking your full potential and opening doors to great success. You are not ordinary, you are extraordinary, and your unique value is what sets you apart from everyone else. Don't worry about trying to compete or fit in; if you embrace your unique value, there is no limit to what you can achieve. Your unique value is most evident in your best performances, and it is the key to your success. Remember that you were born to be extraordinary and valuable. Discover your unique value and explore the endless possibilities that await you!

CONSISTENCY IS A WINNING FORCE

Your peculiarity is discovered from the act of your consistency. All peculiar lives are consistent. The strength of consistency is driven by the force of clarity of vision. Vision is a moving force that demands consistency to accomplish. The winning force of consistency proceeds from the strength of focus; whatever cannot be moved will eventually move what can be moved. Your ability to stay on the right path to your greatness will produce the crown of your victory. Learn to be consistent in all you do; God visits men in their place of consistency and the primary aim of confusion is to take men away from their place of consistency. All that must be rich and successful in life should be consistent in their journey of destiny and shouldn't compromise at all costs.

INTEGRITY IS A CONNECTING POINT TO GREATNESS

It is widely believed that a person's character is a reflection of their behavior. A good person is known for their positive conduct, while bad people are often identified by their negative traits. The path to greatness lies in maintaining integrity, which is a highly valued trait. A person's reputation is often evaluated based on their adherence to integrity. Men of integrity are respected and esteemed in society, and they are believed to have a promising future. The level of a person's self-worth is often associated with their level of integrity.

Integrity plays a crucial role in life, and its importance cannot be overemphasized. People who possess integrity are believed to be rich in value and destined for greatness. It is said that riches are acquired through the path of integrity. Moreover, the sustainability of wealth is closely tied to an individual's integrity. Therefore, it is imperative to maintain one's integrity to achieve financial success.

Furthermore, people who keep their promises and stay true to their words are often regarded as people of value and integrity. God is an excellent example of a being that embodies integrity. His word is inseparable from him, and he is known for his unwavering commitment to his promises. Therefore, it is essential to emulate God's example by keeping our word and maintaining our integrity.

24 Heaven and earth shall pass away, but my words shall not pass away.

(Matthew 24:35)

Each time men become one with their words; their value increases and their reputation enlarges. People will not respect you for what you say, people will respect you for keeping to what you have said; that's integrity.

CHAPTER 6

RICHES ARE HIDDEN TREASURES IN MEN

Treasures are not truly valuable until they are converted into riches. Without giving them value, their worth remains hidden, and their usefulness is not fully realized. The preciousness of a treasure lies in its significance and importance, which are determined by its place of worth. Every person is born with hidden treasures, and it is up to us to convert them into value to increase our productivity. Life is precious, and we must treasure it to preserve it. We can preserve our lives by recognizing the value they hold and protecting them at all costs. We must be careful and mindful of the importance and relevance of our lives, and strive to become a treasure to the world. Only then can we truly realize our worth and be valued by others.

To live a life of value, we must first treasure it. Those who have already done so should live from the riches of their treasured, preserved value. It is possible to preserve our lives by making them a treasure and valuing them above all else. Preservation is more important than riches, and we must prioritize it above all else. To treasure our lives is to preserve them, and to preserve our lives is more important than seeking wealth.

THE IMPORTANCE OF PRESERVATION

1 He that dwelleth in the secret place of the most High shall abide under the Shadow of the Almighty.

2 I will say of the LORD, He is my refuge and my fortress: my God; in him will I trust.

(Psalms 91:1-2)

Preservation is incredibly important when it comes to ensuring your safety and security. Without preservation, it's impossible to protect the things that matter most to you. God understands this and prioritizes preserving our lives before granting us wealth or success. When we neglect to preserve our lives, we become vulnerable to all sorts of challenges and difficulties. It's crucial that we take preservation seriously and make it a priority in our lives. After all, we only get one life, and everything we do and experience affects our well-being. The first step towards achieving success and abundance is preserving your life. All life is precious and valuable, and preservation is an excellent way to save lives. Your life is as precious as you, you must save your life by preserving it.

DON'T USE YOUR LIFE TO LOOK FOR MONEY; USE YOUR VALUE TO GET MONEY.

Many people who lost their lives chasing after money failed to make proper use of their inherent value. A proven way to become wealthy and overcome poverty is by investing in your discovered value and self harvestment from the place of your relevance. Money is best earned when it is attracted through productive value. The essence of a man's life lies in their soul. Those who exchange their soul for money will ultimately face eternal doom. It is wrong for money to take hold of a person. The love of money, which prompts one to do evil things, is the root of all evil. Those who have an excessive love for money tend to engage in evil activities just to stay with their wealth. Those who lost their lives in pursuit of money became slaves to it. On the other hand, those who use their value to attract money should develop Their inner abilities to control it. Don't spend your life chasing money; instead, use your inherent value to attract it. Only people without a sense of value will use their life to chase after money. They will go as far as selling their soul to the devil in exchange for money.

36 For what shall it profit a man, if he shall gain the whole world, and lose his soul? [37] Or what shall a man give in exchange for his soul? (Mark 8:36-37)

UNDERSTANDING THE VALUE OF MONEY

Money has value. The primary value of money lies in its power to facilitate exchange. Understanding the exchange value of money is crucial for wise spending. The value of money should not be underestimated, lest it be abused. Those who desire wealth should carefully comprehend the value of money. Abusing money is tantamount to neglecting its value. The power of money is measured by its value. Those who do not appreciate the value of money should not be given access to it, as money is best left in the hands of those who recognize its value.

PRINCIPLES ON WISE SPENDING

1)   **Do not spend money on things that are not profitable.**

2)   **Invest more and spend less.**

3)   **Spend money on assets more than on liabilities.**

4)   **Do not invest money in things you are unsure about.**

5)   **Invest in yourself at all costs.**

6)   **Protect your money.**

CHAPTER 7

THE RICHES OF GOD IN A MAN

22 The blessing of the Lord, it maketh rich, and he addeth no sorrow with it.   (Proverbs 10:22)

The true riches of God in a man are not limited to

material wealth, as money is just one aspect of it. The riches that truly matter are the treasures that God has stored within every one of us. These divine qualities of God found inside a man are what make him truly rich. Any form of riches that does not come from the divine source will eventually end in pain and poverty.

The first and foremost riches of God in a man is divine Wisdom. It is the principal thing and the foundation of all riches. Divine wisdom can only be given by God and anyone who desires to be rich should seek it first. This wisdom is not to be confused with earthly wisdom that can be acquired, as it is entirely different and is only bestowed by the divine.Another rich gift of God in a man is understanding. It is a spiritual gift that functions from the springs of God's Grace. Those who possess understanding are gracious and know beyond human reasoning and knowledge. It is a gift from the divine to a humble heart, and anyone who lacks it should ask of God who gives to all men liberally.

5 *In Gibeon the LORD appeared to Solomon in a dream by night: and God said, ask what I shall give thee.*

6 *and Solomon said, thou hast shown unto thy servant David my father great mercy, according as he walked before thee in truth, and righteousness, and uprightness of heart with thee; and thou hast kept for him this great kindness, that thou had given him a son to sit on his throne, as it is this day.*

7 And now, O Lord my God, thou hath made thy servant king instead of David my father: and I am bought a little child I know not how to go out or come in.

8 And thy servant is in the midst of thy people which thou has chosen a great people, that cannot be numbered nor counted for multitude.

9 Give therefore thy servant an understanding heart to judge thy people, that I may discern between good and bad: for who can judge this thy so great a people? (1 kings 3: 5-9)

In the Bible, King Solomon was offered anything he wanted by God. However, instead of asking for riches, he chose to ask for an understanding heart. This is because he knew that true wealth is built on understanding. In fact, all wealthy individuals possess a deep understanding of life, which they use to create their wealth.

If you want to activate the riches of God in your life, you must make sacrifices for Him. This is because God is pleased to lift those who sacrifice for Him, as it shows a strong dedication to Him. When you make sacrifices for God, you get His attention, and He will bless you in ways beyond your imagination. So, go ahead and make those sacrifices for God, and watch as your blessings overflow!

GOD'S GRACE IN US IS AN ASPECT OF HIS RICHES IN US

God's grace in individuals enables them to access God's presence and divine abilities. Through Jesus Christ, God bestowed one of the greatest blessings upon the church, which is the Grace of God. Those who are gracious carry the essence of God within them and embody His riches. Grace is a divine gift given by God to those with humble and meek minds.

To be gracious is to be divine, and all divine beings share power with God. Grace exposes us to the riches of God through our inner abilities, and our productivity in God's vineyard is a manifestation of His divine grace within us.

10 But by the grace of God I am what I am: and his grace which was bestowed upon me was not in vain; but I labored more abundantly than they all: yet not I, but the grace of God which was with me. (1 *Corinthians 15:10)*

The presence of God's grace in our lives reveals the abundance of riches that are available to us. There is enough grace within us to achieve great things; we just need to make proper use of it. To find grace, we must submit to and obey God's word. If we remain obedient to Him at all times, He will increase his grace in us, and the more we are enriched with grace, the more sufficient His supply becomes for us.

6 *But he giveth more grace. Wherefore he saith, God resisteth the proud, but giveth grace unto the humble.* (*James 4:6*)

PROSPERITY IS A NATURE OF GOD IN A MAN

Prosperity is a characteristic of God in a Man because God is prosperous in nature, and all those who resemble God are Prosperous. Man is made in the image and likeness of God. Therefore, for a person to be prosperous, they must possess the nature of God within them. This divine nature is what makes a person successful and fruitful. When you have the life of God in you, it connects you to the Rivers of God that flows abundant prosperity, riches, and joy without any sorrow. The first step towards becoming prosperous in life is to have the life of God within oneself. The life of God in a Man flows like a River, such life is an abundant life.

7 He that believeth on me, as the scripture hath said, out of his belly shall flow rivers of living water.

(*John 7:38*)

GOD DELIGHTS IN MEN'S PRODUCTIVITY

1 I am the true vine, and my Father is the husbandman.

2 Every branch in me that beareth, not fruit he taketh away: and every branch that beareth fruit, he purgeth it, that it may bring forth more fruit.(John 15:1-2)

The capital reason why you are alive is to be productive; productivity will bring you to the path of success and discipline will keep you on that path. God will depend on the productivity of a man to bless the man. All that is not productive has been disconnected from the river of God; the divinity of God in a man is evidence of his productivity. All that are productive have God in them. The strength of the relationship between God and man is raised from the Altar of usefulness and relevance. It is how productive you are becoming that will determine the level of attention God will give to you. All productive beings are godly beings. To be productive is to have God in you. The Holy Spirit is the spirit of productivity; the evidence that you have God In you is seen from the level of growth and productivity visible in your life and ministry. Becoming productive in life and ministry is a sign that God is with you. All productive beings are Divine beings.

BE PROSPEROUS

17 Thus saith the LORD, thy Redeemer, the Holy One of Israel; I am the LORD thy God which teacheth thee to profit, which leadeth thee by the way that thou shouldest go.

(Isaiah 48:17)

Prosperity is something that we all desire in life and achieving it is within our reach. It's like a flowing river that we need to be connected to in order to experience true abundance. Anointing of a prosperous person is a key factor in achieving prosperity which can help us exercise our own anointing and grace. With the power of prosperity, we can experience success in everything we do. It's important to remember that prosperity is a sign that God is with us, and reveals the divine nature within us. Failure is not of God, and so when we are prosperous, we are living in alignment with His will. Sacrifice is also a crucial part of prosperity, as it allows us to fully unleash the strength of God's divine abilities to prosper us. In other To experience true prosperity, one must be willing to pay the price and make the necessary sacrifices. Remember, prosperity is within our grasp and we have the power to achieve it. To be prosperous is to be successful and to be successful is to be divine.

1 Blessed is the man that walketh not in the counsel of the ungodly, nor standeth in the way of sinners, nor sitteth in the seat of the scornful.

2 But his delight is in the law of the LORD; and in his law doth he meditate day and night.

3 And he shall be like a tree planted by the rivers of water, that bringeth forth his fruit in his season; his leaf also shall not wither; and whatsoever he doeth shall prosper.   (Psalms 1:1-3)

CHAPTER 8

YOU ARE BORN TO BE RICH

Poverty is not an inescapable fate that is thrust

upon anyone. You are born with the potential to be rich and successful. The earth provides countless opportunities, and the first opportunity you have is to explore and discover your unique qualities. Every person who enters this world possesses something special to offer. Your worth is determined by your individuality. Wealth is hidden within every individual, waiting to be unearthed and utilized. No one is born to be poor, and those who accept poverty as their fate are denying themselves the chance to make a significant impact on the world. Every individual possesses a God-given deposit that can lead to wealth when developed and utilized. You already have everything you need to succeed in life, but you must examine and cultivate your abilities to be productive. Your ability to be productive is a sign of your wealth. The journey towards wealth begins with self-discovery; you must look within yourself to determine what you can contribute to the world. Your usefulness to society is what will determine your greatness.

POVERTY IS LACK OF SELF RELEVANCE

The mistake many people make in life is to search for things they should not be looking for. Pursuing money at a young age without first discovering yourself can lead to a life of confusion and ridicule. Therefore, the first step in life should be to discover your self-worth, as this is what will build your self-relevance. Those who accept poverty as their destiny are often poor because they fail to recognize their own self-worth. Every poor person sits on a goldmine of untapped potential, and poverty is the byproduct of not realizing this potential.

In life, do not rush to acquire material possessions without first understanding who you are and what your purpose is. Self-discovery and self-improvement should be your primary focus, as this will determine your destiny and life purpose. Poverty results from living a life that is not in alignment with who you truly are, and blaming others for your misfortunes. A poor man is a lost man, and until he discovers his true self, poverty will continue to plague him. One of the ways to overcome poverty is to recognize your self-worth, develop a mindset of greatness, and utilize your potential. Those who achieve great things are those who believed in themselves and developed a positive mentality before embarking on their path to greatness. Overcoming poverty is not difficult if you have the right mindset and believe in your ability to achieve success.

YOU CAN CHOOSE TO BE GOLDEN

It's important to discover and understand your purpose in life. Living with a sense of purpose gives meaning and importance to your life. Depending on others to survive will leave a void that cannot be filled. To live a golden life, you must be special and unique in your own way. A preserved life is a golden life, and the earth only rewards those who meet its demands. Being outstanding in life means embracing your uniqueness and living a golden life from a place of individuality. People will respect and honor you for your golden nature, but they will adore you for your unique values. Remember, all golden lives are discovered lives, and they thrive on their unique values.

YOU ARE SPECIAL

Your lies in your Value; your earth importance declares your earth relevance. You are not just special, you are exceptional, and you are deeply loved. You are created in the image and likeness of God, and you are God's masterpiece. Don't allow the challenges of life to define you, and don't accept defeat just because you cannot see victory coming. You possess the divine uniqueness and the divine ability of God in you to do all things. You are the glory of God, and you need to see it and feel it. If your answer is yes, then you are not just special, you are outstanding! Say "I am special," call your name out loud and clear, and say, "I am special." You are the apple of God's eye, and you are unique. Understanding who you are will shape your thinking pattern and position you for greatness. Live from your discovered self and uniqueness, and your true light will shine forth with confidence and courage.

LIVE FROM YOUR VALUE

Living a fulfilling life is not about lacking anything necessary for survival. It requires you to discover your uniqueness and potential to achieve self-value and fulfillment. The key to fulfilling your potential lies in the pursuit of a personal vision with discipline. Your self-worth and self-importance are intertwined with your values, and they are essential for your success. Recognizing your importance in the world is essential to accessing the gate of riches. Your uniqueness is a vital aspect of being a blessing to your generation, and you must discover it to achieve your true potential.

Living a life true to yourself is essential to achieving success. You must live a life of purpose and self-discovery to tap into the resources you need to succeed. When you live purposefully, both God and people will bless you.

CHAPTER 9

RICH DESTINY

To achieve a rich destiny, you must take full

responsibility for your life. Greatness is something that lies within individuals and is a result of their self-discovery. Anything that has achieved greatness on earth has done so for a specific purpose, and you are no exception.

According to 1 John 3:8, anyone who commits sins is under the influence of the devil, who has been sinning since the beginning of time. However, the Son of God came to earth to destroy the devil's works. Actualizing your life's purpose is not an option if you want to live a fulfilling life.

Discovering the actual purpose of your life is the key to achieving greatness. Do not waste your time living a life without direction, living a purposeful life is the only way to preserve your life. Many people wander aimlessly on earth because they are not aware of their purpose. Do not let that be you.

One sign that you have a rich destiny is that the creative spirit is alive within you. All creative individuals are destined for greatness. Being creative means being optimistic and innovative. Everyone is born to be rich, but not everyone is born with a rich destiny. Being rich in destiny goes beyond having money; it means living a purposeful life based on your discoveries. Every discovered life is a recovered destiny. The measure of a life's reward is based on how it was lived in accordance with its purpose. Living a life without purpose is a waste of time and resources.

The destiny of every individual is reflected in what they live for, and becoming rich in destiny is a function of one's bloodline. Do not let your bloodline hold you back from achieving greatness, instead, let it inspire you to reach for the stars. You are capable of achieving anything you set your mind to.

RICHES FLOWS FROM BLOODLINE

Greatness is the result of an advanced bloodline. All great bloodlines advance their roots through their rich destiny. Kingship and rulership are functions of bloodline. One of the ways to determine if you have a rich destiny is to understand your origin's bloodline. It is your bloodline that determines your richness in destiny; if your bloodline has produced rich destinies, being rich will not be difficult. Rich destinies accomplish remarkable feats and leave a lasting legacy in the minds of many generations. Jesus is very rich in destiny, and this greatness can be traced to his bloodline, which is why he is the most popular and powerful man in the universe.

1 And there shall come forth a rod out of the stem of Jesse, and a Branch shall grow out of his roots:

2 And the spirit of the Lord shall rest upon him, the spirit of wisdom and understanding, the spirit of counsel and might, the spirit of knowledge and of the fear of the Lord;

3 And shall make him of quick understanding in the fear of the Lord: and he shall not judge after the sight of his eyes, neither reprove after the hearing of his ears:
(Isaiah 11:1-3)

It is believed that Jesus came from a bloodline of Kings, which made him the King of kings and Lord of lords. Your ancestry can have a significant impact on who you become, as outstanding traits and characteristics can be passed down from one generation to the next.

Therefore, being rich in destiny means having a strong and remarkable bloodline. The greatness of every individual can be traced back to their lineage.

ADVANCE YOUR BLOODLINE

19 The earnest expectation of the creatures are waiteth for the manifestation of the sons of God.

(Romans 8:19)

Every manifestation from a particular place is undeniably channeled back to its origin. Greatness is not just a concept, but it is evident in the people of a great place, and every great man came from such a place. To be relevant to your place, you must advance your bloodline. Every person is born into a particular family to advance their bloodline, which in turn improves their family's reputation and existence.

For example, if you were born into a family of preachers, where your great-grandfather, grandfather, and father were all preachers, then the preaching spirit runs deep in your family, awaiting your readiness and willingness to carry on the task of advancing your ancestors' bloodline through discovery and recovery. You don't need another destiny when your bloodline has already provided you with one. With this knowledge, you can confidently move forward knowing that you have a purpose to fulfill and a legacy to uphold.

1 After six days Jesus took with him Peter, James, and John the brother of James, and led them up a high mountain by themselves. 2 There he was transfigured before them. His face shone like the sun, and his clothes became as white as the light. 3 Just then there appeared before them Moses and Elijah, talking with Jesus.

4 Peter said to Jesus, "Lord, it is good for us to be here. If you wish, I will put up three shelters—one for you, one for Moses, and one for Elijah."

(Matthew 17:1-4)

It is an indisputable fact that Jesus arrived on earth with the purpose of advancing the bloodline of his ancestors. This was made evident during the Mount of Transfiguration, where his ancestors appeared and spoke to him, urging him to continue their bloodline. Let it be known that Jesus brought a superior manifestation of grace and truth, which represented a significant improvement upon the law that was brought by Moses.

17 Think not that I am come to destroy the law or the prophets: I am not come to destroy, but to fulfill.

(Matthew 5:17)

The fulfillment of the Law has confidently introduced grace and truth, paving the way for every bloodline to advance through the confident people of the land. God improves our lives through advancement of his program on Earth per .

GOD GIVES MEN DESTINY FROM THEIR BLOODLINE

The essence of a man is inextricably linked to his source. You are not here to live for yourself, but to live for your source. Your life's purpose is defined by your understanding of your source. To live a fulfilling life, you must live in accordance with your source. The life of your source will beget a destiny that is uniquely yours. There is no destiny outside of your source. God provides men with their destiny through their source, and understanding your source is the key to knowing what you are meant to live for.

7 And the Lord said, I have surely seen the affliction of my people which are in Egypt, and have heard their cry by reason of their taskmasters; for I know their sorrows;

8 And I am come down to deliver them out of the hand of the Egyptians, and to bring them up out of that land unto a good land and a large, unto a land flowing with milk and honey; unto the place of the Canaanites, and the Hittites, and the Amorites, and the Perizzites, and the Hivites, and the Jebusites.

9 Now therefore, behold, the cry of the children of Israel has come unto me: and I have also seen the oppression wherewith the Egyptians oppress them.

10 Come now therefore, and I will send thee unto Pharaoh, that thou mayest bring forth my people the children of Israel out of Egypt. (Exodus 3: 7-20)

To have a destiny, it is essential to understand your life's purpose. When God calls you, it is for a purposeful life, and you must live up to that calling. Therefore, it is essential to live your life with purpose and confidence, knowing that you have been called by God for a reason

The Law Of Process

Living a fulfilling life is an ongoing journey of progress. The importance of progress cannot be overstated, as it signifies personal and collective advancement. Being progressive in life is a matter of adhering to the law of progress which dictates "Forward ever, backward never." Success in life and ministry is intrinsically linked to being progressive, and the true essence of success is encapsulated by the law of progress. Any obstacle that hinders an individual from making progress is an impediment to their success. To make progress, it is essential to have a strong desire to progress, work hard towards it, understand the principles of progress, and take necessary actions to move forward. Without progress, one's purpose in life may remain unfulfilled.

13 Brethren, I count not myself to have apprehended: but this one thing I do, forgetting those things which are behind, and reaching forth unto those things which are before. (Philippians 3:13)

Success in business or ministry requires a confident approach, and one of the most important steps towards achieving this confidence is to learn from past failures. If you are not making progress in your endeavors, it is likely that you have not yet learned from these past mistakes. Progress is a sign that you are growing, and one of the best ways to grow is to avoid repeating the same mistakes that once held you back. The pain of experience from our past failures can act as a guide to future success. Remaining in a place of defeat for too long is a clear indication that you are not making progress in life. To achieve success, you need to be progressive and confident in your approach.

CHAPTER 10

BUILDING A FORTRESS WITH YOUR VALUE

A fortress is a place of refuge. It is a sure place to hide and be safe in the time of trouble. God doesn't build fortresses for men, men build their fortress from their discovered Value. The hiding place of every valuable Man is in the fortress he has built for himself from his Value. The reason why some people are easily destroyed when challenges come their way, is because there is no fortress they have built for themselves. God will be in the fortress you have built to protect you. All Great lives attained greatness from the place of Their hiding which is their fortress. God doesn't protect men directly, you are the one to provide the material for your protection. All that were defeated In Battle were first destroyed from their place of hiding. To build a fortress from your value; qualifies you to become a refuge for others.

SATAN ATTACKS THE FORTRESS OF MEN BEFORE HE DESTROY THEIR LIFE

The fortress of your life is the secret that holds your Life. All Great lives are built in secret and the secret of your life is the foundation of your fortress. It is very precarious to share your life secrets with unworthy people. Every successful life is found by secret, what will sustain your life, is the secret of your Life. Be very careful of people that seek access to your life and progress; they are only interested to know the secret that holds your life and progress and once they discover your secret, your life will be in their hands. Satan attacks men from the secret of their Life. It wasn't difficult for Eve to be destroyed in the garden, the moment she shared the secret of her life with the enemy which is the Devil. The Devil depended on the secret that Eve shared with him to destroy her and Adam in the Garden of Eden. SATAN will never attack what he doesn't understand, so, Each time your life secret is exposed, your fortress is destroyed. One of the ways to achieve uttermost success in life and ministry is to hide in the fortress of your life. The fortress of your life is the secret of your success. Don't discuss your success with unworthy people, it will attract enmity and envy because of the low states of their minds. Great lives are sustained in the power of keeping secrets. To be rich will not be difficult if you are good at keeping secrets. Every secret you know PRESERVES your life and God will always relate with Men that can hold secrets.

YOUR LIFE IS PRESERVED IN THE SECRET THAT HOLDS IT

People must not know everything about you. The only people you should be very transparent with are the people who are ready to share their life and Destiny with you. Don't be transparent to strangers, Until they pay the necessary price to be called family. So many lives and Destinies have been destroyed because they shared Their life with the wrong people. There is no preservation outside secrecy because whatever that is understood is open to attack. The defense of your life is from the fortress you have built from the place of secrecy. To trust people is wrong; I think people should earn your Trust. Don't easily trust people with something you have paid so much to Know. The value of your life is measured in the secret it can uphold. If you make your life vulnerable, it will lose its fortress and strength to defend you in times of trouble. God will preserve your life from the way you are living it. Being reckless and careless with your life is a sign you are ready for destruction. All protected lives built the fortress for their protection through what they know above others. Your life can only be preserved when you are ready to keep it from attack.

YOUR VALUE IS YOUR FORTRESS

It is expedient to build refuge from your value. Selfishness is a characteristic of lawlessness. You are raised to raise others. Your divine ability to lift people from their place of defeat Produces a crown of refuge and fortress for you. God doesn't produce a crown for Men, God wears men the crown they produced from themselves. The people you help today in life will become a shelter for you tomorrow. Don't limit yourself on being Good to people because the Good of Everyman is what introduces their importance. Selfishness in the lives of people introduces them to the gate of doomness and all selfish Men are servants of Satan. Don't use your only life to serve your desires, use your life to make positive impacts on people.

Great lives became Great from the relevance of their impartation towards their generation. The earth is a place of importance and it is your value that will introduce you to the important people of the Earth. All valuable lives wear the crown of honor they have produced from themselves through their Value. Your Value becomes your fortress when it becomes a source of blessing to your generation.

BE USEFUL

Your usefulness is very important. All important lives are very useful to themselves and to their generation. To be useful is to be relevant and all relevant lives shine like the Stars. What will make you outstanding can't be separated from your usefulness. Your usefulness can not be replaced because of the level of its impact. All useful people are forever remembered from the fortress of their usefulness. To be useful is to be an asset and not a liability. Important people will only relate with you from the place of your usefulness. Adam lost his place in God the moment he lost his usefulness before God; it is your usefulness that will keep you around important people. It is your usefulness that promotes your value and all promoted value from the place of usefulness can't be separated from Honour.

In conclusion, to be rich will not be difficult if your usefulness brings your value before greatness.

OTHER BOOKS BY ANTHONY ENU:

1.   TO BE RICH IS NOT DIFFICULT

2.   THE ORIGINALITY OF GOD IN A   MAN

3.   THE   WINNING   FORCE   OF FAITHFULNESS

4.   PRAYER WORKS

5.   THE POWER OF SIGHT

For more information about the book or the author please kindly contact inspirational Library/ Anthony Enu:

Website: http://anthonyenubooks.com/

Email: anthonyenu34@gmail.com